LIGHT AND OTHER OBSERVATIONS

BY MARTIN CATHCART FRODEN

Published by Borland Ceilidh Publishing
Kilmarnock
WWW.BORLANDCEILIDHBAND.COM

ISBN: 978-0-244-73180-9

To contact the author: -
MARTINCATHCARTFRODEN@GMAIL.COM

Version: December 21, 2018 3:41 PM

LIGHT AND OTHER OBSERVATIONS

BY MARTIN CATHCART FRODEN

BORLAND CEILIDH PUBLISHING • KILMARNOCK • SCOTLAND

Supported by the Arts & Humanities Research Council through the Scottish Graduate School for Arts & Humanities

Contents

Foreword

It was my first visit to Newhailes House on the wintry morning of the interviews for the National Trust for Scotland poetry residency. My feelings on approaching the property were similar to those described by James Crawford in his essay entitled The Lost Estate: 'Now it wasn't looking at me as through me, towards something distant...Perhaps it was gazing all the way back to its birth.' I am sure that this is a common sentiment, of a building being conscious of its history, its purpose and repurpose through time. The residency offered the opportunity for a writer not only to respond to National Trust for Scotland sites as his or her muse, but also to, perhaps, explain why we apply human-like attributes to edifices and landscapes.

When Martin Cathacart Froden was appointed as the poet in residence his presentation on Newhailes spoke of 'Curlicues and tendrils, from Georgian foundries / To warm hand, curious footfall, long gaze.' Touching, exploring and observing the properties and the collections held within them would be a source of curiosity and wonder.

Rachel Campbell-Johnston, writing in The Times in March 2003, said that, 'Poetry can open up a world which lies within and yet beyond the ordinary world – like one of those secret chambers behind the library panelling.' In a similar fashion, the poems produced by Froden inspired by this residency open up extraordinary worlds. Hugh Miller's Birthplace Cottage in Cromarty, Culloden battlefield near Inverness, Robert Burns Birthplace Museum in Alloway, the Tenement House in Glasgow and the island of Canna are amongst the locations across Scotland that Froden has visited and responded to.

Froden deftly applies a variety of writing styles and techniques including prose, imagery, erasure, list and some of his own innovations. For example, in the poem "Mannerism" reflecting on a painting in Pollok House, the picture frame itself is embedded in the piece, disrupting and disorientating the reader. An effect that suggests that walled art and objects contained within historic properties can somehow throw a visit into disorder.

In his poem "Swim / under / lux" Froden uses the handsome description of 'a salt-distorted sky'. In many ways the themes found in this collection become distorted; time, language, memory are formed and reformed in 'a lullaby of progress' ("Fossil Fields"). This is a collection that offers new insights with each reread, in a similar vein to revisiting a historic attraction where we delight at a new detail registered about an artefact or research uncovered about a person or event. I hope the writing inspires you to experience the National Trust for Scotland places for yourself and see if you can spot many of the references and moods evoked by Froden's poetry.

Asif Khan
Director, Scottish Poetry Library

Notes from the Author

Over the last year I have had the privilege of being the National Trust for Scotland's Poet in Residence. The people I've met have been more than welcoming, taking time out of their busy days to show me around and to tell me things I would never have known. And knowingly or less so, they have always given me enough to translate into poetry. I've seen my role as an innocent bystander, one who is allowed to come in and glimpse objects, overhear stories, extrapolate and benignly misinterpret. Hopefully one that has been able to shine a different light on some of the sights on our doorsteps, wherever our doors are.

I have wanted to come to these poetic objects, these houses, islands, castles, and homes, slowly. And to leave slowly, which has meant train and cycling for most of the visits. I wanted to approach the properties taking in the land and the weather, the way they are situated, and to come upon entrances, grand or unassuming, in an older way than the car affords. In terms of logistics that has meant furious scribbling in a pocket-sized note book, hunched over a cup of tea on a returning train, often with ink stains and the black kiss of a dropped bicycle chain marking me out. With notes to look up the globus cruciger, the birth date of Agnes of Dunbar and the number of smoke stacks on smaller CalMac ferries – all red herrings by the way. With history and the present whirling around me, slowly finding their way to the page.

It's been an outstanding year and I've seen corners of Scotland I never thought I'd see, and for that I will be forever grateful. I hope you enjoy the words.

Martin Cathcart Froden

Moirlanich Longhouse

Outside Killin, with sheep and a substation for neighbours, a shard of another life. A long home with just a partition between livestock and people. Outside, my flask and I thought about time and life. I had driven up feeling the kindly hills look at me. I drove home, happy to be alive in the 21st century.

Stirling
Killin
FK21 8TS

Light

As a feather, as a yoke
Passed on from
My father. Light as
A white lie to my
Mother when I came
Back at first light

Family

A sister and
A brother
One fallow
One a mother

The grain
In mother's land
Grew to
Horse-steadying hand

Between whisky cupboard
And Bible chair
Trying to match boy-locks
To neighbour's hair

Maybe no one asked
Could be everyone knew
A burbling burn of rumour
Probably just those two

A child gifted
From above
He, the last owner
The most secret love

A brother
And a sister
Cold nights
Sometimes warmer

Hugin and Munin

I remain
Chained to my brother
He is as different
From the sun
As I am
As is possible

In flight
Him West;
Me East

His beak gleams
His coat greasy
We serve

The one-eyed God
Suspended in the sky
Moving East to West

Slabhraidh
Never slack

Directions

A82 /
A journey impossible in a day
A85 /
In the mind
A827 /
In the lifetime of the hus
FK21 8TS /
Unbridgeable time to
56°28'38.2"N 4°20'09.9"W

Almanac leaves

Peeling back brittle layers of time to the first cuckoo
Of the year, to a Venn diagram of smoke and ash

To the clip-clops of piebald fieldstones, encased by
Seasick angles and local maths, draughts kept out

By hessian and tulle, to barley scones and
Warm eggs palm-cupped, probasti me

A nail

Snip and onto the
Next They throng in
Water Roughshod measures

Notches from a father's
Hammer Handled with care and
Working rage The day filtering
Through fingers

Prayer-like A clinker longship
Of Vikings An angry cat's
Cradle Teeth out

Consummate

I put half an avocado in a ditch
That'll confuse the local insects
I put miles and miles
On the odometer
Sitting, passing nature
Coffee too hot
Coffee gone cold
Maybe I should cut
My flat in half and only use a third of
My things/clothes/the gained time on
No matters other than the Bible
How can the brain cope with
This and Tokyo? I could be there
Tomorrow if I hurry

Longhouse
Or just house
Or just home
To the siblings and a
Boy, begotten or
Immaculate. A little
Messiah of the Glen
Or not

Of the road

The old summer walker
Heather, horn
His stories canter

Axe took a finger
Pot boiling antler
Ashes smoored over

We'll see him next year
The old summer walker
Gluing far to near

Holmwood House

This was the second visit I made in my role as poet. The house, hidden away in Linn Park, has been through many guises, but remains perfectly proportioned. I cycled up the hill, the White Cart Water burbling below, ate a cheese sandwich in the weak sun until the keeper's dog found me.

61-63 Netherlee Rd
Glasgow
G44 3YU

The unsung floorboard

Waxed on knees. Waning from sapped pine to birch white.
Veined. A recumbent copse painted in sun and moon.

Rounded timber, planed for comfort.
Upside-down barrel vaulted by time.

Nailed into place by tired hands.
Lifted for treasure, for mis-gurgling boiler.

From core to rim eyelets, smaller to bigger.
Groaning and contracting with seasons.

And a paraffin heater.
Resin and grain measuring storms and time.

Of vines and twirling ivy

The organising principles
The Greeks around the table

Blind Homer tuning his lyre
Turning his eyes
Away from hands on others' knees

The table is set for ten.
Achilles, Briseis, Hector,
Veronica, Patroclus, (pass the Salt please),
Calliope, Andromache, Gaea,
Helen, Ajax and Hermes (more wine?)
In the kitchen the Pleiades are shouting

An altar of food
The floor a chessboard of hardwood
Human lives the set pieces

The organising principles
The Greeks soon under the table

Holmwood home

(1:1.414 ratio)
A paper
A house perfectly proportioned
Wind roses flower in corners
Not a house that makes you feel important
Or a house that makes you cower
It's a house that makes you feel human
A circle of glass and masonry
The radius of the Earth's curvature
Wooden antennae commune with the celestial Greek
The lines as close to the Minoans we'll ever get
Calm, confident, on the squat and earthly side
An A4 turned horizontal
(1.414:1 ratio)

The maid has returned to see

Pop rivets and ceiling roses
A confessional cat flap
And three new electrical standards

Door lintels from a fabricated Crete or Egypt
Too high for any pharaoh to hit his head on
Too narrow for the bull monster

On kitchen flagstones a nod
To the winking gardener then back
To the scullery: Turtle soup to be ladled

Light and shade and Umbrian browns
And the blue of Athena's coat
Spread over port and gravy

Smoke detectors, slim cigarettes
Peeking down out of daisies
There's a man behind the wallpaper, she says

Brodie Castle

How many rooms, over how many floors? Over how many years? An old Z-shaped castle, re-imagined over and over, and its brand new play park. Imagine being the last person in line, the one who sent the letter to the Trust. And there's a letter too in the library from Robert the Bruce. Couldn't capture this castle, there was so much of it.

Forres
Moray
IV36 2TE

Un objet d'art come undone

Fruit rots, cadavers stink
Saints swear and massage bunions
Concubine yeast-bellies swell, cherubs bicker
Labels bleed spelling mistakes and ceilings rain plaster
Bug-eyed allegorical children, lost/not lost in the forest, give up
Mary's had enough and horsehair's not
Enough for this sagging chair
Cowherds' panpipes crack, copper stags relieve
Themselves into sand-polished urns

Complications

Every hour is as long as the next
Whether still in bed
Or moving in bed

My hour as short as Earl Soandso's
Here pictured on top of his warhorse Chronos
His eyes lightning bolts, as are mine
From an out-of-date prescription
His foot in stirrup
While I'm thesaurusing 'stirrup' with quick screen-fingers

But what if there were 72 days to a month
9 days to a week
13 melodies to play for 12 on-the-hour chimes
11¼ seconds to the minute?

If Sirius or an annual algae-bloom was our leading light
Would his life span and/or mine have felt different
Would the stirrup [no other word found] have fitted him better?
I've spent 552 Soandso minutes standing
here trying to work that out

Curatorial practice

Carpet knife to 12by6 oil
Canvas to cut out the family
Dog from the chase scene to
Frame him better

By degrees

High enough for lacquer not to crack
Low enough for vermin to go elsewhere
Wool jumpers pulled down over knuckles
A workforce in doubled socks
Crystal cobwebs outside
Inside cloudy breath
    A house in hibernation

Eiderdown never fails
If spin cycle's full of
Tennis balls cut in half
Bring a sturdy pet
To warm you
A hand tied mat like this
Can't be bought for money
A textile mille-feuille on
Uneven floorboards
Or hung on walls, stemming the
Corpse-cold, layer on layer
    Soon summer, soon

Glass

Light and time in an awkward polka
Wan from milky windows

Propane heater keeps panes
From breaking

Clouded panes, lead cames
Overlooked by bevelled edge

An equator in linseed oil
Lamp black, spirit

Thinner than a fingernail
Longer lasting than dynasties

Frail too: cobble,
Ladder's shoulder, myopic bird

Turning light viscous
And time riverine

Hugh Miller's Cottage

Right by the tidal firth, just past a long row of cathedralesque disused oil rigs, a little house where a giant of mind lived and worked. Worked so hard with his hands and his pen. A beautiful setting for what was maybe a complicated life. Fossils and new ideas are not opposites I found.

Church St
Cromarty
IV11 8XA

Racing thoughts

Hugh is *Glistening*
in an enamelled coat,
as if beautifully japanned
Collecting in the haar

Awkward
Is the privateer's blood
Always on the boil

Sails billowing
Stranded on the storm beach
Wind-side on

His keel grinding
Leap tides reveal
Boat-like animals,
furnished with oars and a rudder

Italics from 'The old red sandstone, or, New walks in an old field: to which is appended a series of geological papers read before the Royal Physical Society of Edinburgh' Miller, Hugh, 1802-1856. Publ. 1858

The flexible straight edge

Chisel held at a
52° angle
Same as Giza
The sun-slant

1 cubit from trilobites and legislation
Mason marking corners
Seven straight lines
From mallet to wallet

Teasing evolution
Out of rock
Putting scalloped back in
And dates for * and †

A sum of ergo

How long is a mile
Who did we send to school today
How wide your thumb
Who would better the world if we didn't

The girl whose depthless intellect can't fit
The dull hard-working boy
How deep's your embrace
Under water

What do you see when you close your eyes
Who did we send to school today?
Round peg
Square hole

If train A leaves the station going 49 mph
and train B leaves 73 min later going $12^6/9$
mph faster, how long will it take train B to

Hill of Tarvit

This was my first assignment working for the NTS. I was suitably nervous, and early. I wanted to arrive like people have for a long time, so I caught a train to Cupar and walked a long way up a hill (the busy A916) that seemed to never end. It was worth it and after the visit, walking back down the hill in the gathering dusk, I wrote everything I could.

Cupar
KY15 5PB

The house on the hill

Tick-Tock, hickory clubs hitting balls
Missed shots and curses from the undergrowth
Royal and Ancient

Tick-Tock, the picture framer busy on site
Figs, melons, doves, an eagle, dead or dying
Pigments and ruse

Tick-Tock, curling stones clicking into place
Of billiard's break
Tallies and scores etched in sandstone and memory

Tick-Tock, shooting hounds on hardwood floors
Outside and inside only a pane apart
And I count only the bright hours

Siblings

The boy slips out of bed. Joints not yet creaking. Sighting.
A smashed pane of glass will wake sister. But a straight
shot, over hedge, rolling up to surprised-at-nothing
sheep. Another swing out through French doors,
soldiers in yolk and tea together, marching up the
lower lawn wearing crampons in preparation.
/
All these boys. Clubs and mallets and rackets and balls. All
these boys decanted onto the grass, to aerate. Allow the house
a deep breath. All these boys crammed into the summerhouse
on castors, following the sun, girasols on industrialist's rail.
/
The last woman, a lonely sister. Upstairs, the last hours,
starched Marie Curie. Her best rooms kept for those
bitten by the Crab. She gifted her home and her life
within it. Just like that. As if life was just a game.

Sunday bag

Putter
His careful collecting, poring over catalogues. Luxurious and
fecund said in one breath. I like this and an investment, said in
the next. Completing the collection. Nothing is ever complete
once you start looking. The cupboard needs filling, the walls
a population. After a long day's stalking, tasselled lamps
burning bright. A note dashed to Groningen, a rogue curator.

Jigger
The Hill-stranded ship filled with Kolf-on-ice. Three living
still-lifes, captured and wild. And now the absence will
make the heart. The muted colours of wealth, accrued
from tobacco and favourable winds. The restrained
gilt dulled, polished back to life by Florijns.

Mashie niblick
Rules, scores, manuals. The fleeting and deadly
importance of game and forest's game. The clock has
spoken from the wheelhouse of the mansion. The
table is laid under old gazes. Silver ship on wheels, a
partridge decapitated for pouring. A leap year, a new
flower for the family rose. The outside brought inside.
And tomorrow too.

Pictures (no longer) at an exhibition

Shrouded and empty.
Where heroics used to be.
A triptych of restoration.

Elbow grease and Ruper magnifier.
Egg yolk, pigment. Radio 3.
If they could tell us what we look like to them.

Faces parading, our clothes outlandish.
Dutch masters need sleep too.
Limelight'll cost you, old muck removed, new make-up applied.

Nailed back up on the rostrum come winter.
Framed in red tape while white-gloved, squinting, rapeseed oil.

Begin a day's toil on sable or sabre.
Which is worth more, the picture or the frame?
Spot Breugel. Spot false decanter. Spot Ming.
Is that a newsprint cigarette?

Newhailes House

Here, in a bitterly cold ante-room under the stairs, with an odd door at an angle staring at me, I was interviewed and introduced to Asif, David and Ylva – and the Trust. It was a house in winter, hibernating, waiting. A library to lose track of time in. But then I had to cycle back to the train, to the rush of it.

Newhailes
Musselburgh
EH21 6RY

Newhailes House

The sun's slow fireworks display
Benevolent spectral, moving through the row of rooms

Curlicues and tendrils, from Georgian foundries
To warm hand, curious footfall, long gaze

Motes of time floating, settling
Meeting you halfway there

Silk long lost, not danced in since Napoleon
Honoured, held up to the light again

The marble still swirls the same
A duck's egg, cracked into a copper pot

Nothing has been altered
Everything has changed

Ivy like mascara, inexpertly applied
Fibonacci on proud display

Pitter-patter and Somme limp
Cane squeak, the wheeling of tig

Tactile and taciturn, seconds blaring
 Down a corridor of time, loud as angels' brass

Child's toy

Flakes of paint, an eye lost
And not button-replaced
Worn smooth, loved
And discarded
Five times a day
If displaced
       the veil of the heavens
       would be rent in twain
       from the top to the bottom;
       and the earth would quake

If found, after:
Overwrought parents,
Flushed nannies,
Candlelit human chains crisscrossing the garden
Their only thank-you would be sleep
Proprietary half-smile
Unimaginable love, tucked into bed just so
                            Sleep.

Spring ball

Almost all the way to
All the way to
      Helen
The stroke of midnight at my temples
      Earring touching bared shoulder
      White marble in a quarry
Something in my throat
      You move your head
      To polite doubt
      Recognition of
Feet sore not from dancing
Staring-standing
      Then you come
      An inch, a dimple
      Closer
A breath lost can never be regained
      A breath lost
      Dancing with
Dancing for
    The long way home
    The long way home

Fickle fortune

The past is a place
And it has sunk
Into the foaming

Landed
Shells
And
Knowing

The bow wave
First smiling
Now mewling
The water's not receding

The past is a place
And it is lost
In the gloaming

Hermiston Quay I

I've come across from Glasgow on the train so many times I feel like I know the people in the local Tesco where I've lost my wallet (twice). Behind a retail park, close to the motorway is a very modern building for what is mainly a historical pursuit. Open, alive, and bursting with energy, this is the mothership. And it has a café that sells everything Tunnocks.

National Trust for Scotland Central Office

5 Cultins Rd
Edinburgh
EH11 4DF

Collecting habits

Uncaressed for 200-odd, odd years.
A forced, cellophaned celibacy

Schoolchildren's aspartame gazes
Bouncing off curves and plaque
Kneel before this week's golden calf

Touched by so many hands,
then *Please Don't Touch*
Stroked by trembling conservator, cotton-bud probing

Next week: An intercooler from a clapped-out Fiesta
The week after that [insert reading device]

Vestige

In a water-cooled industrial unit, the size of Ormskirk
Noughts and half-crosses assembled
The bay, overlooking white, toppled, marine skyscrapers
Ferrying/fetching folk to/fro St Petersburg
As in the Alps, and filmatisations of the Ten Bells
The cloud has come down, resting around ankles
Growing in size, kin to mushrooms
Corrugated shed, exposed girders, fans and numbers
Rows of Terra

> Screenshot Oct 15, 2018, 21:28:20
> A katyusha/hellfire through the walls
> Erasing profiles and constitutions.
> A dainty finger hovering over Enter
> Opening times, maps, pictures of
> pictures of children playing croquet
> Gone, code unravelled. Not even a ruin
> to sift through

Worst case scenarii

Trestle tables, pump thermos with instant
coffee. 'Milk and sugar over there pet'
2-for-1 stalls upended by mutt looking for
Gravel-kissed sausage roll. A parish car boot sale
or
Russian, or worse, English, oligarchs
Objects dressed up as family history
On mantelpieces in second homes
Divorced from taste, couriered into wealth
or
'Here boy!' Leg of chaise longue gently
Chewed to splintered. White elephants on display
Raffle tickets doing the rounds, choice of:
Curry Buffet or Globus Cruciger
 or
Landfill for A96 slip road. Chopped up for
Brownie firewood by gentlemen dads
Call our highly skilled team on 0800 305 305
To discuss your skip hire requirements
or
The public petering out
Chipboard over windows, interior bats
In empty bridal chambers and ballrooms
Steps of lethargic guide-guards echoing
or

Hermiston Quay II

Minne-Spiegel

How tiring to be human
And manically collect
To see time quickly nibble
At matter and intellect

How delicious to be living
And quietly reflect
To see light change to darkness
Blanketing our mess

A dorm of fearful squirreling
Of trinkets, silver, rhymes
Inconsequentíal as a typo
The buzzings of twelve flies

How chaotic to be human
And placidly forget
To misnomer, misplace, discard
Matter and intellect

Anemoia

The nostalgia for a time you've never known

And the next

I saw the woman look at the tiara, or whatever it was, and I saw her joy, desire, realisation And I sought her look, trapped her eyes as they veered off the icicles of value In the hope that her lingering shadow, afterglow, retinal impressions, would in her mind associate the object with me It didn't Which is good I'm not a thing I'm quite affordable really and rarely guarded by infra-red I saw the woman look at the next thing And the next

Culloden

A battlefield on every Scottish schoolchild's lips, lingering in the minds of history buffs. A spell spoken through the crackly PA of coachloads of American tourists. A serene, quiet building, reminiscent of a crematorium or war memorial, on a field that could have been any field, but isn't. I came here on a cold day when the swallows were still shy. I hadn't expected to be as affected as I was.

Culloden Moor
Inverness
IV2 5EU

The battle of Culloden

And then the pipers begin to play

████████████████████████

Crows peck and tear, flies fatten up

Plaque to the living and the dead[1]

Eilidh Jonston,
Mathieu St Leger,
Molly Cautley,
Garfield Weston,
F Dürkheim-Ketelhodt,
David Lumsden,
Charlotte Beatrix Pitstra,
Michael Black,
Charlotte Orr,
Charles Edward Stuart,
Mabel Featheringham,
William Augustus,
Mhairi Brennan,
John Mor MacGillivray,
Emilie Laforge,
John Fraser,
Tara Beal,
Alexander Grossett,
Elina Koristashevskaya,
James Drummond,
Jenny Cameron,
Alexander Fraser,
S C Lobban,
Ensign Dally,
Lucy Blair,
Me,
You,

,

---

1. Names of museum patrons, decision-makers, battlefield casualties, my office colleagues

Weathered

Blade
Of grass
Sharpened steel
Broken on rib cage
In parlour rooms
Blades
Of grass dripping
With rusting water

Fossil fields

Beneath my bed I found
A tangle of black fangs
In a lullaby of progress
The derrick loudly bangs
More, more, more

The dead don't care, but the living should.
How come we haven't solved this?

The hills look down the same
Heirs of skylarks flitting
A field is just a field
Somewhere else is ending

The dead don't care, but the living should.
How come we haven't solved this?

More, more, more
To rid myself of trouble
I kept one toothless viper
And when I lay my head to sleep
I hear its oily whisper

Elysian fields?

6 Apr 1453   –   29 May 1453
16 Apr 1746   –   16 Apr 1746
21 Feb 1916   –   18 Dec 1916
6 Aug 1945   –   9 Aug 1945
1 Nov 1955   –   30 Apr 1975
18 Mar 2011   –   present
11 Jan 2032   –   31 Sep 2033

Mecum omnes plangite

Robert Smail's Printing Works

The absolute joy of words and writing and art is so clear here. It's a working place, where sentences come together like tiny miracles. David and I struggled to spell our names correctly in setter's blocks. It's no secret I love this place. My incantation: may future generations know the smell of ink.

High St,
Innerleithen
EH44 6HA

Cardiogrammar

The flight of your eye

As regular as heartbeat

    The

                         flight

of

             your

  eye

As irregular and irrevocable

As the heart's wish

Ctrl+P

This is a tpyo, a topy, a TYP0
A poet's play is a printer's pain

Type AB(C)-positive

Births, deaths, social teas
Church minutes, fixtures

Capturing life is the
Printer's alphabet
As (il-)logical as qwerty
As α, β, γ, δ

Under bare lightbulbs
There's a song for every speed of the Heidelberg
Out of the stream and onto ream
The lung-like machinery

Count your blessings if
You can count 10 fingers
At end of day

At night a Bavarian limestone
Around your neck, and rickety
Eyesight from 4pt (lower case)

Glory be to God on High
Sale of potatoes this Saturday

White space

Guillotine, scissors,

p e r f o r a t i o n s,

cut-outs,   .

       What's not there

       as important as

       what's there

Forgetfulness, distractions,

Mistakes, bad luck, the radio,

Mechanical mishaps, an off day,

       ,   .

Consigned

ﺵ

From greengrocer's apostrophe
To apothecary's latin
[sic]
Comes in handy

ƺ

From guillemets flown
To ligatures gone missing
Nimble fingers flit
In the d's workshop

ꞢⱯ

Their
There
They're
It's its its'

Ⅎ

From foundry to
Facsimile to
Faxed to finnished [sic]
Comes in handy

ש

Dead diphthongs
Umlaut, &c
Jumbling in
A drawer

🌿

Raster

A prismatic translation
Of informal constraints
Majuscules and minutæ

Where ink bleeds
Into 1s and 0s
Serifs to Pixels

M = square
N = ½ square
Letters and numbers
  Put to bed

On paper

And we shall judge among the nations, and we shall beat our
swords into ploughshares, and our spears into pruning hooks

                                        And into type

Cygnus-white
Burnt-black
Cumulus-white
Night-ink on
        off-white

Meaning onto
The frost-like (papillose)
Surface (cellulose)

        The weight of paper
        Equals the weight of us
        { Finger-smudge
        Light as a kiss }

Island of Canna

180 miles later, after trains over gorges and through the best Scotland has to offer, over choppy seas with birds and white-faced day-trippers for company, the locals slumbering over their paper from the mainland, I was once again still. An island is a stronghold and a home and this one is a pearl as well. I was given heartfelt hospitality and empty beaches to tread. Canna will be with me forever. Thank you.

Isle of Canna
PH44 4RS

La propriété, c'est le vol?

Me and my wife own a flat
The bank owns 94% of that flat
My share is 2.9 m2   (5.8m2 / 2)

Who owns an 11,300,000m2 island?
Tides making it smaller
Then bigger, all the time

The flat is absolute space
The island isn't
And what do you do with all that rained-on,
Craggy, heartwrenchingly difficult,
Beautiful, space?

Canaigh

Folk and their songs
Seals and their stories
Waves come and go
Quick and eternal

Time and its mien
Kittiwakes a'wavering
Love can never dull
In a seagreen home

Anna recording

Waxed jacket
Hat on the ground
Equipment set up
The children kept quiet
 Anna, just a farming girl
 Singing her songs
 Like she would anyway
  Then going back to silage
  And children
  And arms red from sun
  And salt water
While the wax cylinder
Is brought into the house
Swaddled like the bairn
  That never arrived
  Listened to
  Catalogued
  Loved and kept
Anna thinking nothing of it
Her voice
In the ether, in my ears
 Travelling on waves of time
 The moments between
 Click and voice
 Song's start and finish
  Time spooling

Past / future / tense

For gate: If you opened it, shut it
For island: If you shut it, open it up

Island song

The scale
The seal's welcome
The sails
The song of Home

The scales
The ivory and black
And the wind
Will bring you back

Muted

Closed shutters
    The house is sleeping
        What is it dreaming about
          Who's in its beds
            What songs
            And small-hour talk
        Is it replaying?
      A house A pile of stones
 A home A melody
   And rhythm A hearth
     A heartbeat
        Punctuated by meow, meow
         And the hiss from
            Tape recorders
              Rolling

Inherited typewriter galore

JKJLP121LJK my frustrated fist would have written. Punched, sacrilegiously. Then pling, kettle, fag from housecoat pocket. Maybe after lunch she too would JKJLP121LJK and give up for the day – or persevere until jumbled became slate waves and the ribbon twin spool emitted whisky-warmth. From morning, the moon's cuticle showing, to evening, astral sliver winking again.

Freed from the blinking cursor, sat and sat. Same as anyone reeling out their mind via slow fingers. Reset the paper, just so, finger resting on the carriage release lever, hoping the wind wouldn't rip off the roof, maybe that it would. Faint smell of porpoise oil drifting up from newly serviced machine guts.

Five lucky pressings of the space key, then into it. Into the foaming waves and splintering timbers. Their lobster-fingers, her fingers too, cold no matter what. When the guide looks away I softly write JKJ

Swim / under / lux

So quiet, an end
What a way to start life
There must be a way to cheat

To look up
At a salt-distorted sky
One more surface
Between me and cloud cover

Within grasp
What a choice
Breaths coming going
Not coming

What a luxury to come out
Canna, island nation
Wrapped in water

Margaret Fay Shaw Campbell

Carried
to Nova Scotia and
Old Scotland

Family names
Piled up like
Home-spun shawls
Around her

Tenement House

I had a day out on my bike where I travelled in time and class from Pollok House in the morning to the higgledy-piggledy streets of Garnethill in the afternoon. That one city can house these two lives is amazing in itself. The ordinary life lived here, is made extraordinary. Everyone is a secret recipe of time and impressions, of expressions and keepsakes. This gas-lit life is no exception.

145 Buccleuch St,
Glasgow
G3 6QN

(Re-)Collect

(Re-)Collect
I just remembered I forgot
I must remember not to forget
I mustn't forget, can't
This is a reminder to

A note-to-self in oil on canvas
In coal and pinned-up gas bill
Half-remembered, half-forgotten
A threnody in Meissen or BHS

A string around our finger
A mnemonic device from paper
Books in a row, a phalanx of know

Esker

On the seventh hill
Of the seventh hill
Right next to a synagogue
> Overlooking
> Secular and sacrosanct spires
A Caryatid
A Morris Column
A woman
> With the pitch and yaw of living
Wattle and daub
Coat rack and doilies
Her space made her space
> With brio
> Then baulking
Who decides to not go with the times
Day's work over
Tired hand
> On worn close newel
Who decides to ignore the passing of time
Passing of horse and car, omnibus, Concorde
To collect receipts
> Coupons, theatre programs and
> What a relief to ignore the passing of time
On the hill a woman

A stitch in time

Light as a cloud in a bucket of water
Heavy as responsibility
Stretching, making space for the unspeakable body
Hemming in what can't be on display
Displaying what should only be imagined

Violet as a dream, quick and slow
Fine in the looking glass
'But people will see it mirrored'
Right or left shoulder up or down or neither
          or both with this or that brooch
Ballooning, as if plunged into the Clyde
Stiff as ice on a curling pond
Metered out, exact dimensions, exact invoice
Not altered more than three times

White as a sheet only whiter
The girl, But the dress;
'I'll make it purple, so you can wear it again pet'
Pinching, propping up, conserving a shape
          part fantastical, part flesh and blood
The young woman
A memory even as worn
A shape the grown, with hips, would remember
But not miss, no longer Miss

A quiet querencia

Best room kept for
       Kept clean
The best secrets are
       Kept secrets
       Are they?

Best rooms are
       Kitchens and bedrooms
       Surely?

Best kept for
       New Year's Day
       Special visitors
       Suitor(s)

Best room kept for
       Kept clean

Compartmentalised & keyed in

How many words a minute dear?
Is, am, I, ~~wsa~~, was, it
                vs
jackhammer, pozzolanas,
extemporized, zygapophyses
isopropylcyclohexane

Milk, coal,
Soap, vinegar
A place for everything

F next to G
just below R above V
A space set aside for

A spacious home for one
Because made for
5-6-7
A keyboard made for
26 plus ampersand
And accoutrements

Typing like playing the piano
Can't do that now, Rheumatism
Only sometimes on the bedcovers
Für Elise for the NHS (still a novelty)

Waltzing (1928)

Men and their
Long suffering
Significant
Others

Horse-trampled suffragettes
Calling all dancers
Cruickshank,
The Polka and the Skank

A slow Glasgow kiss
A stubbled chin
Cobbles coming
Loose like molars

Women and their
Undue patience
Daily-made, insignificanced
Calling everyone and all the others

Sisters, brothers, lovers
The strong and the pushovers
Vanderbilt,
The Dainty and the Clydebuilt

A quick shuffle
On dappled floor
Barrowlands
Borrowed time

Home

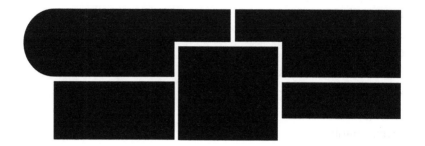

Robert Burns Birthplace Museum

The land surrounding, the lives encompassing a house are inextricable from the actual building. And in this case Burns' words are threaded through with the land. I found this an excellent, complicated exhibition, then I found the humble house. On this outing I was on a new (now stolen) red bike. I'm not blaming the bard.

Murdoch's Lone,
Alloway
Ayr
KA7 4PQ

Secular saints

Rabbie, George Best, Alex Arctic Monkey, that guy you see in Tesco sometimes. Men, meh. Vanity (Latin vanitas, from vanus 'empty'). Are we filling their cup for them? Are they reaching for a top-up even from heaven, Hollywood, aisle 9? The (self- / other-) aggrandising male. How many children with how many women and how many unclaimed, undetected, uncreated by chance / luck / lunar movements? Raise another glass, raise another fatherless child. Ploughmen hammering seeds into furrows far and wide. Men, meh.

Lingua franca

The written
The spoken
The consecrated
The broken

The imagined
And the real
The beauty of an honest tongue
It steals

The spoken
And the written
Built by those who don't
Give a sh*t about
Either of them

Who is RB-ing today?

Who speaks / writes for the country?

Famous in his / her lifetime? Sleeping rough, then suddenly under eiderdown? Sleeping around, sleeping later and later in the morning? Where is Scot(land)'s future? Where is language produced and (re-)imagined? Created, lived, embodied, forgotten, true, of scant importance? On a bus, online, in a bed (just after), in a sobering-up unit, in a field, in a field hospital amputating? Probably not where I am.

 Where is this daunting and everyday task performed (in a country of longwinters and shortsummers)? It is a daily, oblique occurrence. With tongues and fingers. With touch and sound that lingers. With giving and taking, communicating, creating. (A rhyming, by chance).

(A work (**a word**) that is **created** (fixed in tangible form for the first time) is automatically protected from the moment of its creation and given a term of copyright protection enduring for the lifetime of the artist plus an additional 70 years after the artist's death. In the case of a joint work prepared by two or more artists (a wee chat) who did not work for hire, the term lasts for 70 years after the last surviving artist's death. **Everyone's an artist.**

Word-births in Young Offenders Institutions, on an island, in a fight over something stupid, whilst slicing open your thumb. In insults (meant or not), in the academy, in the playground, via onomatopoetic misunderstandings, misspelled scrawls, at the fitba, in the hame.

TL;DR
Who shouts for the country? A woman for a change?

P

-olemic

-olitical

-otato

-olitely

-reservatory

-assive (aggressive)

-ushkin's brother?

-roto-Scots

-roblematic

-owered by rhyme (only?)

-atriarchal

-otato, the humble

-ell-mell to -all Mall

-ettles (elsewhere)

-oor Jean

-roduct (the -oet, the -oetry)

-rotracted -athos

-eripheral nation (discuss)

In William Burnes' orchard

In William Burnes' orchard, Scotch Bridget, Clydeside, Bloody Ploughman, Thorle Pippin, Cutler Grieve, East Lothian Pippin, Maggie Sinclair, Mere de Menage, Stobo Castle, Lass o' Gowrie, King of the Pippins, Katy, Red Devil, Tam Montgomery, Discovery, White Melrose, Tower of Glamis, Scrog, Beauty of Moray, Widow's Friend, Seaton House, Stirling Castle, Love Beauty, Fiesta Red Pippin, Ribston Pippin, Scotch Dumpling, Hawthornden, Belle-de-Boskoop, **by the left-leaning byre**

Burns – a retrospective

Component parts:

Saudade
The missingness for an absent something or
Someone one loves
Which carries
A repressed knowledge that
The object of longing might never return
And a slight suspicion
That there is a past that never was
A nostalgia+

Sedimentation
Of wurds / cultural memory / folk
An OED O.D. /
past-words / pass-words
Obituarial leanings
(Save us from the)
deathinition of a nation /
definition of a Language

Schemes (rhyme)
Poesy: a rustic novelty
His sound ideas:
Our festschrift continuum
Twa tongues:
The hero with a thousand tongues

Sociolect
Dialect / dialectical materialism (abbr. Diamat)
The rough diamond found himself in a land-crinkle
Received pronunciation and rejected vocabularies
The argot now equals ingots

Lex ignis fatuus

Possession is eleven points in the law
And they say there are but twelve

But the tongue (mother- or father-) is thinly veiled
A whirling, flickering flame
Matchstick held to spirit

Ownership is easier to maintain
If one has possession of something

The spontaneous
And decomposed
Leaps to something composed
Off the cuff, on the train

In the absence of clear and compelling testimony
Or documentation to the contrary, the person in
Possession of words is rightful

Assimilation is 11/12ths
Expression 12/12ths of a language

The Hill House

I pedalled, slowly, up the hill from the train station. Rain, befittingly, falling, trickling inside collar. Helensburgh has its social strata visible in elevation. At the top of it, an artwork in roughcast. The lines, the squares, the details, prescribed down almost to the hairbreadth by the two! designers. I was alone in this home, in this statue with four walls, for many hours that morning. When I came out life seemed chaotic. The rain was still falling, but not in straight lines.

Upper Colquhoun St
Helensburgh
G84 9AJ

Gesamtkunstwerke

The house is a
t
 r
e
 l
l
 i
s
To suspend on
Expand the perfect square with

The south facing proposition, an
a
   t
      t
          a
              r

A house statuesque

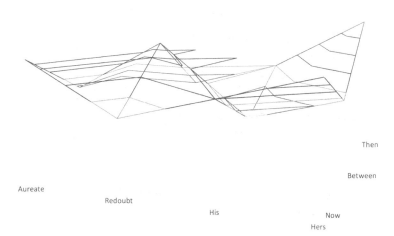

Then

Between

Aureate

Redoubt

His

Now

Hers

Decidious

Daughter, daughter, daughter, daughter, son
The flowers of most species have five petals
(Jean, Ruth, Alison, Agnes, Walter)

Collectively the sepals are called the calyx
        the outermost whorl of parts that form a flower
Collectively the children are called the Blackies
        the whirl of legs, elbows, hair, that form a family

Daughter, daughter, daughter, daughter, ...
One by one leaving home, the way it should be
(Hulthemia, Hesperrhodos, Platyrhodon, Rosa, ...)

Sneewittchen

The russet winter apple
Uneaten on a branch
A drop of red suspended

The drawn and quartered dwelling
Empty on the hill
A glass and concrete moment

The cubit

Stranded on Mount Ararat

A palistrophic ocean liner

Come to rest on a hill above the Clyde/Gareloch charybdis

A structure to weather-the-winds

Pollok House

Surrounded by Glasgow's well-heeled art lovers, I walked on thick carpet and well-worn ceramic tiles. There's a little bit of Spanish madness on the Southside. The kitchen, the size of an Italian piazza and as marbled, is still turning out huge scones. I walked up and down the staircase while trying to work out if the neighing outside was real or an echo from a yesterday. I still don't know.

Glasgow
G43 1AT

Reisekamera

No offence, but did
Everyone look exactly
The same (unless
somehow grotesque)
At the turn of
that century?

Men in hats, women
Undernourished, forearms
Knotted, primly knitted

Siblinged in silver chloride
Monochromed, silver-templed
Preserved in/on gelatine

A gene-pool stagnant
Or the unsteady hands
Of the photographer

Mannerism

A fettered owl. Eyes older than time. Flirting with thematic
leather spines. Questionable lineage. And the painting too.
I think she knows her way around. In contrast to the life below,
she's stilled. An ordinary painting of a famous person, or an
extraordinary painting of a nobody? On entry, eye contact,

before reading,
leafing too.
and reception,
a painting,
perhaps?
you come back
Δομήνικος
(Κρής) or
Angussola,
peak or peak
fur wrap. Fur

half-way through
Dress, provenance
maybe. A subject,
a painter/ress,
Above all: When can
for another sitting?
Θεοτοκόπουλος
not, Sophonisba
or not. Widow's
of affair. Lady in a
coat, no knickers?

Once there were six Goyas

2 here   (where?)
2 there   (Prado)
2 missing   (a brother, a gambler)

Young king lantern jaw

Unable to chew, unable to procreate, trussed up in
silks, standing on the (shaky) shoulders of Carolingians
and Merovingians and other semi-fictitious ancestry,
consanguineously ruling an empire The darkening blood
will blot out castles and armada, bread and sweet water

There were

> 1. those who spoke to the king and
> received his reply with their heads covered
>
> 2. those who addressed the king uncovered,
> but put on their hats to hear his answer
>
> 3. those who awaited the permission
> of the king before covering themselves
>
> > But in the end it didn't matter
> > (Cumulatively deleterious effects)
> > (No heir)

Culzean Castle

A fine, unrelenting rain was colouring the sea grey, nature's lacquer. I said Hello to the staff and auxiliary hands busy polishing the armoury and working out the table setting for the Burns supper. I left my umbrella in the hollowed out, taxidermied, upside-down crocodile (yup!) and lost myself in the optical illusions of the house (carpets, feet, staircase, etc). Later I walked mile after mile outside, listening for echoes from the sea caves below.

Maybole
KA19 8LE

Margaret Erskine of Dun

–A filament broken–Conspiracy of sudden night–
–Mug-clutching dark–The dancing influenzaess–
–Constructed from dust–Descend, skip–
–Her sepulchral kiss–Has me

The walled garden

| Half of use | Half to amuse |

18Hz*

ppp   forgotten memory

pp   Piper lost inside hillside, and his dog

p   sallow spectrogram

mp   wind a drone, a bag-lung exhaling cavernous dirge

mf   vestibular system straining,
weather system pounding coast

f   whale, elephant, rhino, giraffe, okapi,
alligator sing in infrasound over vast distances

ff   notes born in severe weather, surf, lee
waves, avalanches, earthquakes, volcanoes,
bolides, waterfalls, calving of icebergs, aurorae,
meteors, lightning and upper-atmospheric lightning

fff   traumatic transmissions are articulated over time
not only through social sites or institutions but also
through cultural, political, and familial
generations, a key social mechanism of
continuity and renewal across human groups **

---

* The resonant frequency of the eye is ~18 Hz. Optical illusions can be caused by your eyeballs resonating.

** Gabriela Fried Amilivia

Time: apparently an irreversible succession

Les lieux de mémoire
Pre-aged arch
In lieu of history
The ruin
Calque of expressions

Dieu et mon Mer
The waters come in
Twice a day to look at the castle
A saline whirlwind
Caressing trunnion and quoin

~~*L'hantologie*~~ *L'hantologie*
Seven spirits moving in
Apsidal precession
The armillary
Swirling

Hidden / under

Scipio's eight children
His manumission

Smugglers' caves
Servants' walkway

Lord Summerisle
Ruling over bent wicker

In depth, in debt
Waters' harvest
Castle's keep

Culzean

Over time
The letter   ſ
(used in Older Scots)
Became confused with   z

The Stores

In a warehouse so secret I lost my way, a waiting room for objects. Some art, some not so much. The tea served in reception was heavenly for this hatless cyclist. The units are kept cold, so cold that fingers slip when they try to write number sequences. So fragile is our link, that once a scrap of paper is lost, once someone forgets, once a method or technology is outmoded, once your Granny passes.... I had another cup of tea, before I made sure to forget where I had been.

Sverdrup

Circadian rhythms are regulated
      by genes, which provide chemical feedback

      (I like this. I want to buy this. I no longer like this.
          Or; I will keep this until bequeathment)

    On circatidal, circalunar, circuitous routes through the city
to end up here – Influx / Efflux – – Inhale dust / Exhale frost

 In and out of storage containers, the
Ins and Outs of Keeper's tenet
 Mover's blankets – – – The colour of a Leith sky

All in a day's work

FromG20 8RT on08.45 (6FBY2018 Class25911 STD1731995034
Visa4751401056766402 (SORT070344 ACC31124899))
ToEH6 7RE CageH11 Code931 ItemC1820.99.1589

& C1820.99.1589, 931, H11, EH6 7RE, on13.45(R/T) toG20 8RT

Inheritance law in Scotland

The current law and practice

This section of the briefing outlines some of the key terminology associated with the law of succession. A more detailed glossary of terms associated with the general law can be found in Annex A of the Scottish Government's 2015 consultation document (Scottish Government 2015c). In inheritance law the deceased person's property and possessions are called the estate. The people or organisations that will benefit from the estate when it is distributed are called the beneficiaries. Where a person makes a will he or she is sometimes referred to as the testator. His or her estate is described as testate. Legacies and vesting A legacy or a bequest is a provision in a will giving some benefit to the person or organisation named in the provision. There are various different types of legacies, for example, a pecuniary legacy is a legacy of a sum of money. A legacy or bequest is said to vest when the beneficiary acquires a right to it. In almost all cases, this is at the point of the testator's death. However, sometimes vesting is postponed by the deed creating the legacy to another point in time. The role of the executor and of confirmation The person who manages the process of gathering in the estate, administering it and distributing it to the beneficiaries is called the executor. Executors usually get their authority to carry out this task from a legal document known as the confirmation which can be obtained from the local sheriff court. However, confirmation may not be needed for estates where banks holding funds belonging to the estate are prepared to release funds without it. There is also a streamlined procedure for obtaining confirmation to small estates (which have a total value of less than £36,000) (see further Scottish Government 2015, p 10). A person may name somebody in his or her will where he or she wishes to be the executor. The technical term for such a person is the executor nominate. On the other hand, an executor dative is an executor appointed by the court. Such a person may be appointed in a variety of circumstances, including where there is no will or there is a will but no proposed executor was named in it. In most cases an executor dative will be required to obtain a special type of insurance, known as a bond of caution (pronounced 'KAY-shon'). An executor dative may also be appointed where the proposed executor refused or is incapable of taking on the role or where the person appointed dies before taking up the post. The deceased's spouse or civil partner is exclusively entitled to be appointed executor dative if he or she inherits the whole estate under prior rights (1964 Act, section 9(4)). There is nothing in the general law which stops an executor being a beneficiary. In fact, in practice, an executor may be and almost always is, one of the beneficiaries, sometimes the sole beneficiary. However, where a solicitor is an executor it is a breach of his or her professional ethics for him or her also to be a beneficiary (Macdonald 2001, para 13.101). An executor is subject to the fundamental principle that he or she must not allow his or her own personal interests to prevail over the interests of the estate. So, for example, he or she is not allowed to purchase assets of the estate, unless this was clearly authorised by the testator or, subsequently, by all the affected beneficiaries (Macdonald 2001, para 13.100-13.102). Trusts and trustees A trust is an arrangement whereby one party (the trustee or the settlor) passes ownership of assets to a trust to be used for the benefit of others (the beneficiaries). The trustees run the trust for the beneficiaries. Trusts can be created in wills. For example, they might be used where a testator wants his or her children to inherit under his or her will but not until they reach a certain age. A trust allows the deed of vesting to be postponed until the children reach that age. Perhaps confusingly, even where there is no specific trust created in a will, executors are treated for most legal purposes as trustees too. Accordingly, they are subject to the legal regulation associated with trustees. If a person dies without leaving a valid will, then, on his or her death, that person is described as intestate (as is his or her estate). The law provides default rules which say who should inherit if somebody dies intestate. These favour the deceased person's spouse or civil partner and also provide some protection for the deceased's children (see further below at pp 12-16 of this briefing). Disinheritance and the role of legal rights When a will aims to exclude a particular person from inheriting any of the deceased's estate, the will aims to disinherit that person. Where there is no will, a person also may be disinherited through the normal application of the rules of intestate succession. In Scotland it is not possible to make a will entirely disinheriting your spouse or civil partner or your children. This is due to the concept of legal rights, explained in detail elsewhere.

124

Broken not disposed of

G8 G7 G6
 So meone's gran's second
favourite cat's *second favourite*
cushion

29.1 ↑ 29.2 ↑↑
 ↑
 John Duncan
 Removals
 20<u>6.8.2a</u>
<u>Urgent / Items marked for</u>
 <u>framing</u>

<u>H65/ KE</u>
B53. B54. B<u>55.</u>

Re-cane(£600-700)

2012.419 /*B53. B54.* <u>B55.</u>

<u>Pamela   Young Bequest</u>
<u>TS.219</u>

<u>The Shore Porters Society</u>
1 Baltic Place Ab erdeen
 99.1585

 ~~Prince Philip III of~~
~~Spain, Accession~~   no 73.43,
Brodie Castle

2 **07.827 Clock**

207.84 9   Dish
207.9 06a Tureen

Came ron, Rubislaw
Terrace

207.844 ⟶ .856

Keep away from   direct
sunlight   *versus* Remove
 number and ~~discard~~

 Auctioneer/Charity
(other) *vis-à-vis* Attach_{ment}
/Detachment

Archiving

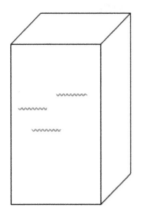

Effects / affects

Mahlstick
Bessie MacNicol's
In a bucket full
Of fag ends and umbrellas

Chronistic
Unsung debutantes, unhung chandeliers.
Square tonnes of yesterdays, numbered and forgotten.
Here a Subterranean, antiquarian traffic jam

A  Ω
Archive's relation to Object. All's revelation to Nil.
Object's reduction to Figure.
Observe a Beginning, the End

Acknowledgements

I want to thank Dr David Hopes and Ylva Dahnsjo of the National Trust for Scotland, and Asif Khan of the Scottish Poetry Library, for their support, and the Scottish Graduate School for Arts and Humanities, especially Professor Dee Heddon and Anna Scott, for making this project a viable reality, and in the same (long) breath, also the Arts and Humanities Research Council, and the University of Glasgow.

I want to thank Gen Harrison and John Grant for their help and editorial input, and my wife Lucy for her keen eye and sharp wit, as well as my children Elias, Alma and Mika for both taking the mickey out of me for being a poet and for being catalysts in so many ways.

About the Author

Originally from Sweden, Martin has lived in Canada, Israel, Argentina, almost Finland and London. He is the winner of the 2015 Dundee International Book Prize with 'Devil take the Hindmost' (Freight 2016) as well as the 2013 BBC Radio 4 Opening Lines competition with 'The Underwater Cathedral'. To date Martin has appeared at a number of literary festivals including the Edinburgh International Book Festival, AyeWrite Glasgow, the Dundee Literary Festival and the Ullapool Book Festival, both as a writer of fiction and as a poet. His short stories have been shortlisted for a number of awards, including the Bridport Prize and the Bristol Short Story Prize.

Martin is currently working towards a practice-based doctorate in Creative Writing, Criminology and Architecture at the University of Glasgow. His studies fall within the broad themes of space, place and literature. He lives in Glasgow with his wife and three children.

BORLAND CEILIDH PUBLISHING, SCOTLAND

DID2412500

L - #0079 - 110119 - C0 - 210/148/7 - PB - DID2412500